I0085240

Prairie Boomer: Farm Boy Memories

Other Works By Brian Hesje

Prairie Fisherman: Fishing Memories
Paperback ISBN: 978-1-9994418-6-9
E-Book ISBN: 978-1-9994418-7-6

Thoughts on Thinking
Paperback ISBN: 978-1-9994418-1-4

26 Thoughts on Leadership
Paperback ISBN: 978-1-9994418-2-1

Why Save Your Golf Balls?
Paperback ISBN: 978-1-9994418-0-7

Prairie Boomer: Farm Boy Memories

BRIAN W. HESJE

PRAIRIE BOOMER:
FARM BOY MEMORIES

Copyright © Brian Hesje, 2021

All rights reserved. No part of this publication may be reproduced, stored in a retrieval system, or transmitted in any form or by any means, electronic, mechanical, photocopying, recording, or otherwise, without written permission of the author and publisher.

Published by Brian Hesje, Edmonton, Canada

Paperback ISBN: 978-1-9994418-6-9
eBook ISBN: 978-1-9994418-7-6

Second Print: January 2021

PAGEMASTER
PUBLISHING
PageMasterPublishing.ca

CONTENTS

INTRODUCTION   7

1. WINTON PIONEERS   9

2. FARM FAMILY   21

3. MORE ABOUT FAMILIES   47

4. WHAT WE DIDN'T HAVE   63

5. SCHOOL DAYS, SCHOOL DAYS   65

6. FUN DURING FARM YEARS   83

7. THEN THERE WAS CHURCH   91

8. REFLECTIONS   95

Introduction

On a tour in Florence, Italy, where we saw the statue of David, the guide asked us, "Did you know that the year the sculptor Michelangelo died was also the year Galileo was born—and the year that Galileo died was also the year Sir Isaac Newton was born?"

I didn't know, but the years were 1564 and 1642! This made me decide to check my own history. I was born in 1946, the year John Maynard Keynes died. He was a famous economist who was born in 1883, the year Karl Marx, another famous economist, died. I, however, did not become a famous economist. What I did become was one of millions of people born between 1946 and 1964, a group that became known as the "Baby Boomers." The Boomer generation became the largest generational group in North American history, until the Millennial generation in the 1980s and 1990s recently surpassed them.

You likely know more about Baby Boomers than you do about Karl Marx or John Maynard Keynes but are unlikely to know what it would have been like to live as a Baby Boomer growing up on a farm on the prairies of rural Saskatchewan, Canada. *I do!* So this is my story. For history to exist, the events must be recorded and believed. History can be recorded and may be believed, but the stories still might not be true. People can remember events differently and may choose to talk about some things, but not others, which can cause our recordings of history to change.

In *Prairie Boomer*, I'll be telling the truth about my growing-up years on the farm to the best of my ability, as far as my research and memory allows that to happen.

My purpose is to describe how, by living on a farm in a world rarely more than 30 miles from home, I learned how to have a successful career and a happy life. The opportunities that became available for me would have greatly exceeded the expectations my grandparents dreamed of for their descendants when they left Norway for a new life in Canada.

Now that I'm retired, I realize how ironic things can be. When I was a boy fishing, I'd look up at the airplanes and wish I was in them. Many times in my career when flying somewhere, I'd look down.

I wished I was fishing back in the river that ran alongside our farm.

So, here's the story about our family and what life was like in that simpler time.

1

WINTON PIONEERS

I t appears to have been my destiny to live in the Winton District in Saskatchewan. Canada was founded in 1867 and needed settlers for the Western prairie land. In 1871, the government enacted the Homestead Act. Its passage meant that any male, aged eighteen or older, or any widow who was the family's sole head, could purchase a homestead of 160 acres for only $10. To gain title, you had to clear a number of acres and build a home. Land was to be farmed, not hoarded.

In 1884, after the Dominion Land Act survey was completed, prairie land was divided into townships and sections. Each township was six square miles and contained 36 sections, each comprising 640 acres. Each township had two sections designated for schools such that no child would be farther than four miles from a school. Winton School District was one of thousands of such prairie school districts in Saskatchewan. Education was important to the settlers and the country.

In 1877, George Agnew was born to Irish parents in Smith Falls, Ontario. In 1879, Margaret "Maggie" Wilson was born, and in

1904, she married George Agnew. My future grandparents had two daughters in Ontario: Alma Elizabeth in 1907, and Mary Dorothy in 1909. In 1907, George's brother Bill had moved to Winton, Saskatchewan and filed for a homestead. In 1910, my future grandparents decided to move west to escape the damp Ontario air that was a problem for my grandmother's asthma. Grandpa filed for a homestead in the Winton district, and in 1912, my mother Ada Pearl was born in Prince Albert. I grew up not knowing that my Grandpa Agnew was a pretty successful farmer and a school trustee who often offered room and board to teachers. Nor did I know that my mother attended Winton School until grade eight, just as I did. Only it was in a building that was replaced a half mile west in 1949. My grandparents lived for over 40 years only two miles from where I grew up, and I never knew it.

I did know my mother's older sister Alma died very young. As a boy, when told of this, I thought she was a small child when she passed away. I didn't realize, at that time, "young" meant different things to different age groups. "Old" always seems to mean someone ten years older than me. Alma actually died in 1929 at the age of 22. As the story goes, Grandpa Agnew was by her side when she pointed upward and said, "Look at that! Isn't it beautiful?" He saw nothing, so the family believed that she had seen heaven. Alma was buried in a cemetery in the town of Kinistino near Birch Hills, but I know not why.

In 1928, Grandpa Agnew wanted to retire and asked my parents to move back from Connell Creek to the farm and rent his land. In 1944, my grandparents moved to the city of Prince Albert. It was only about 30 miles away, but you had to cross the river by ferry to visit. It was the first time they ever had electricity or running water. Grandma Agnew passed away in 1958 and Grandpa Agnew in 1960.

As a child, I didn't know the reason my father would jokingly say, "A Swede is a Norwegian with his brains missing." Decades later, I discovered that Norway had gained independence from Sweden in 1905. Ironically, the same year Canada created the province of Saskatchewan. This was the first time in 400 years that Norway would not be under foreign rule. And although this was a welcome transition, in the 1920s, Norway was struggling economically, and in 1927, about twenty percent of the workforce was unemployed. It is likely that my father's parents and grandparents had resented the Swedes and passed those feelings on to my father. Dad would only say this jokingly and never displayed any negative feelings to Swedish people. It is difficult for me to imagine leaving your family and country, knowing you would likely never return, but that's exactly what Bestapa ("Bestafar" is Norwegian for "grandfather") and Bestamo ("Bestamor" is Norwegian for "grandmother") did. And he never returned, but she did after he passed on.

My Bestapa, Johan Arnt Hesje, was born in 1894 in Norway. In 1898, Karen Kverneland was born, and they were married in 1916. They had six children in Norway: John, my father (1916, born in Hoiland); Tannes (1918); Kaari (1920); Johan Arnt (1923); Lars (1925); and Carrie (1927). In 1928, the family boarded the Stavengerfjord in Stavanger, Norway to cross the Atlantic Ocean to the famous Pier 21 in Halifax Nova Scotia, Canada. On the entire trip to Canada, Bestamo was sick, so Bestapa had to take care of her and the six children.

Historical records at Pier 21 record the arrival of my grandparents and their six children. Pier 21 was a seaport immigration location in Eastern Canada that was in operation from 1928 to 1971. The Hesje family would have been some of the earliest immigrants to use the facility to enter Canada. These documents reflect our name as "Hesje" and my father's age as ten. That, at least, is the history recorded in the official document, but actual events are different. Our surname was spelt "Hesjke" when they left Norway, but Bestapa dropped the "k" so it would be easier to spell. It wasn't! Bestapa declared the grand sum of $25 as all his cash. In my opinion, they took more risk than any of their descendents. My father was born in 1916, so he could not have been ten in 1928. When I got a copy of the original document, I called my father and told him of the mistake. His response was, "It was half fare for those ten and under, so my father stretched the truth. It wasn't right, but I don't think I will get caught now." He was right, because by then, over 50 years had passed.

The journey was not over in Halifax. Their final destination was near Brancepeth, Saskatchewan. A train ride with the Canadian National Railway for 4,300 kilometres or 2,671 miles took several days. Once arriving in Brancepeth, it was a five-mile trip on a horse-drawn buggy and lumber wagon to the home of my Bestamo's sister. Dad unknowingly had travelled thousands of miles so he could meet and marry Mom.

Archival material from the Canadian government shows that in the early part of the 20th century, Saskatchewan was the settlement of choice for many Norwegians. The family was greeted by relatives and friends who spoke their language and would greatly assist them in adjusting to a new country.

Adjusting to a new life was not easy. They came to Canada expecting more opportunities—not easy when arriving shortly before the economically depressed "Dirty Thirties" began. During the 1930s, many countries around the world were suffering from serious economic challenges with Canada being among the worst. Millions of people in Canada during that era in history were unemployed, with many of them going hungry, even homeless. Although no single cause could be identified, there was also a horrific drought in the prairies.

Throughout these incredibly difficult times, my family never became homeless, nor did the family suffer from hunger. The importance of family, neighbours, hard work and doing whatever was necessary became firmly instilled in the family values. Renting land to farm was necessary to survive.

Early settlers had arrived at the Birch Hills, Brancepeth, Winton, Lake Park districts much before 1928, so no "homestead land" was available for the family to buy. It took ten years to accumulate the $1,000 necessary to buy a quarter of land 70 miles away in Crooked River. The property had a house, yard and lake to provide water for the livestock. It was their home for the rest of their married life until Bestapa passed away in 1970. Bestamo passed away in Saskatoon in 1987.

The adjustment to life in Canada was more difficult for my father than his siblings. He had completed four years of school in Norway and had to start over in grade one, because he couldn't speak English. He often told me how embarrassing it was being so much older and bigger than his classmates. Math was especially frustrating, because he knew the answers but couldn't communicate them. He completed five grades in three years, and in 1931, at the age of 14, he quit school to leave home to work to help support the family. My aunt told me that on his last day of school, when walking away, he called back to the teacher by her first name. She called him back and gave him the strap. A story he must have forgotten, because I never heard it from him.

Working for various farmers at such a young age turned out to be a blessing for Dad. These jobs resulted in his getting to know Mom and also the farmer whose farm he would ultimately buy. Both sets of my grandparents lived through difficult times. They saw many changes during their lives but little opportunity to enjoy them compared to their descendants. Transportation became better. Roads improved. Electricity became available. Telephones came into existence and then radio—and then television. It would not be right to forget and not be thankful for their sacrifices, so I could have more opportunities than had they!

Hesjke family leaving Stavanger in search of opportunities

Lars, Bestapa, Johan Arnt, John (Dad), Kaari Tannes, Bestamo, Carrie

Pearl (Mom), Grandpa, Gramma, and Dorothy Agnew

Pearl and John Hesje's wedding picture

First home of Mom and Dad's at Connell Creek

Walter Karlsten farm purchased in 1946

Grocery store and post office in Winton

What Things Cost in 1946

Car $14,00.00
Gasoline: 21 cents/gal
House: $12,500
Bread: 10 cents/loaf
Milk: 70 cents/gal
Postage Stamp: 3 cents
Stock Market: 177
Average Annual Salary: $3,150
Minimum Wage: 40 cents/hr

Cash was scarce, credit cards non-existent but prices low

2

FARM FAMILY

My family history is firmly entrenched in farming. Both sets of grandparents were farmers, and their families before them were also likely farmers. My parents lived on a farm most of their lives, and I spent my first eighteen years on a farm. I also had two uncles who farmed and two aunts who married farmers. I had two uncles who were Lutheran pastors, one uncle a blacksmith and an aunt who became a teacher and married an RCMP officer. Lots of relatives were farmers or married to farmers, as were most friends.

During my youth, I knew the school nurse, my dentist Dr. Reid and teachers. I never knew a doctor, a lawyer, an accountant or a business owner. All my friends lived or had lived on a farm; a very sheltered life. My parents never discussed their youth or how they met, their wedding or living on a homestead at Connell Creek near Crooked River. They never mentioned that they had lived for six years on my mother's parents' farm, but here is what I have pieced together.

Mom lived in the Winton district all her life except for a couple of years, when she went to high school in Prince Albert. Dad left home at age fourteen to support himself and worked on various farms in the area for a salary plus room and board. One of those farms was where Mom lived and another a farm that he eventually purchased. In 1936, at age twenty, Dad filed for a homestead at Connell Creek. He would have paid $10 for 160 acres of land. In the summer of 1937, with the help of his dad and brothers, he built a log cabin and began clearing the land. What their early married years together at the homestead were like will forever be a mystery to me. Apparently, though, they attended dances, and my 93-year-old uncle tells me that Dad was quite a "high stepper." This is interesting, because later in life, our parents didn't permit dancing and never allowed us to participate.

On December 3, 1937, the highlight of Dad's life, by his written account, was when he married my Mom, Pearl Agnew. They lived at Connell Creek for only a year before Grandpa Agnew asked them to come back to Winton and rent the farm. I had always thought Grandpa Agnew had not thought Mom had won the prize when she brought Dad home, but the facts indicate otherwise. He could have rented the land to Mom's older sister Dorothy and her husband, but didn't—he rented to Dad. Regardless of why Grandpa Agnew made the choice he did, once my father was in Winton, he had a two-bottom plough, an eight-foot single disk, a ten-foot drill and eighteen feet of harrows, all horse-drawn.

In 1939, my brother Clayton was born, and four years later, in 1943, my brother Morris was born. In 1944, Dad sold the Connell

Creek homestead for $1,000—100 times more than he had paid seven years earlier. He bought his first Case combine for $1,268. He harvested over 650 acres with it the first fall. He told me he almost earned the cost of the combine doing custom work during the first fall that he owned it. Dad was not afraid of risk or work!

Walter Karlsten had a very nice farm on the banks of the South Saskatchewan River. It was only two miles from Grandpa Agnew's farm. Everyone wondered who would buy it when he decided to retire. According to my father, Walter had been so impressed with his work ethic as a young man that he wanted him to buy the farm even though Dad did not have cash for a down payment. True or not, three weeks after I was born, September 24, 1946, my family moved to the Karlsten place along the river. My brother Murray, born July 17, 1950, completed our family. We now had birthdays each of the last six months of the year. Our birthdays were: Murray's in July; Morris' in August; mine in September; Dad's in October; Clayton's in November; and Mom's in December. Mom was four years older than my father, and it was very uncommon for the wife to be older. Not once did we celebrate my mother's birthday. I don't recall celebrating my father's either. My mother never even told us when hers was. My parents also never discussed the Norwegian language, and it was never learned or spoken at home.

Although electricity was not widespread on farms, in 1946, the farm already had electric lights. This was accomplished through a wind charger that charged six batteries stored in the basement. In 1948, it was replaced from the twelve-volt system to a 32-volt system, which required sixteen batteries and a power generator.

This system gave enough power for a fridge. My dad remembered his first "COLD" drink from the fridge. What an improvement over the ice box. Days without electricity were not the good old days.

My earliest memory at the farm is of sitting on the floor and twirling the dress of my cousin, who was helping Mom wash dishes. Mom washed, and Leona, her niece, dried. Dresses of the day could be twirled by a person—or by a child. I can recall how it made people laugh, and I laughed too. This is not a clear memory, because it is one that happened when I was very young. My first date-specific memory was in July 1950. I would have been three years, ten months old. My mother was in bed at her parents' house in Prince Albert with our new brother, Murray. Beside the bed, on a chair, was a box of chocolates. My brother Morris and I were certainly more interested in the chocolates than in Murray, and we shared them. The chocolates, I mean. Four for him, one for me.

Another early memory firmly etched in my mind was the summer of 1952, when Dad was building a new aluminum machine shed. During construction, he fell nineteen feet from the rafters and landed on the harrow drawbar. Although I wasn't yet six, I can still remember walking with Dad to the house. He never went to the doctor!

Since I was three years old when we got indoor plumbing, and six when the farm got electricity, I have few memories about the farmhouse before we had both. But I do remember the structure of the house and the layout of the farmyard in a good amount of detail. Our farmhouse was built very close to the riverbank. So close, you could throw a stone into the water from the back door. The house itself was a two-story structure with an unfinished basement. The house was always painted white except for a period of time when it was green. The back door faced east, and we always used this entrance. It had stairs going directly down to the basement. The basement had a large cement cistern. We hauled water up from the river to fill the cistern for our needs. There was also an area where we could wash up and leave our dirty clothes after a day working. The furnace was in the basement, as was a coal room. This room was used to store potatoes after we got an electric furnace and no longer needed storage for coal. The wall of the cistern had numerous shelves that were filled with canned fruit and vegetables.

The back door had another short set of stairs going up to the main floor into the kitchen. The kitchen counter and cupboards faced east, so Mom could look out the window at the river when doing dishes. Although she could see the river, she could not see the spot where we swam and fished. The kitchen had a fridge, an electric stove, no natural gas on the farm and of course a kitchen table that could seat six. The south side had a window looking out toward the garage and barn. The main floor also had a hallway at one time that separated the living room and a guest bedroom from the dining room. Dad removed the walls, so we only had one large room and the guest bedroom. The veranda was the entire length of the house on the west side and could be entered from the living room from inside and from the front door outside. The road to the farmyard was west of the house, and it seemed strange that we never used the front door. I guess it was because the veranda was unheated, and in the winter, we entered a warm house from the back door. My mother didn't like the veranda much, calling it the "fly catcher" because it attracted hundreds of flies. The plan may have been to spend summer evenings watching the prairie sunset. That I don't remember, but I have fond memories of reading comic books there in the summer sun. Murray and Morris also enjoyed comic books, with our favorite ones including Archie and Jughead, Superman, Dagwood and Blondie, Roy Rogers and Dale Evans, and many more.

To get upstairs, you entered a staircase from the living room to a landing, turned right and climbed a few more stairs to that level. To the left was the chimney and master bedroom and a large closet with a storage area. Straight ahead was a small bedroom where two of the brothers slept. To the right was a third bedroom where the oldest brother at home slept and a bathroom with a tub but no shower. We were more likely to have a bath weekly rather than daily. For some reason, the light switch was on the outside of the bathroom. Each of us had many visits to the bathroom when someone turned off the lights!

The driveway of the original road was to the west of the veranda. We seldom used the sidewalk to the veranda and along the south side of the house. My mother always planted flowers on the south side of the house. North of the house, three maple trees were planted with the horseshoe pits next to them.

Directly across the road to the west of the house was a very large garden. It was protected by maple trees on all sides except the west. Half of the garden was planted each year and the other half given a rest and kept fallow. Raspberry bushes and rhubarb plants separated the two halves. We grew potatoes, carrots, beets, cabbage, lettuce, radishes, onions, peas, pumpkins and cucumbers. Food was eaten fresh in the summer, and in winter, we enjoyed canned vegetables and fruits. Although not grown in the garden, we also picked saskatoon berries, blueberries and chokecherries, which could be eaten raw or canned or made into jams and jellies. It was amazing how the land and domestic animals provided us with a variety of vegetables and meat as well as milk, cream and butter.

My father was never afraid of change, and a result was that old buildings were replaced as demands changed. Old, rectangular small granaries were replaced with round steel bins that required much less shovelling. The barn was demolished when milk cows were replaced with a corral and a cattle feeding operation. The fenced area for pigs disappeared, as did the pigs. The only building to survive, other than the house, was a garage that was destroyed by fire in 1959 but rebuilt on the same site. That garage exists to this day. Another feature of the farmyard was a road from the barnyard to the river. The road was used by the cattle to drink at the river in summer and winter. It was also used to drive the truck down to the river to haul water or ice blocks.

Animals played a very important role in our family life. I never remember us not having a dog. Tippy and Joe were two such pets. Joe was a little black-and-white dog that broke his front leg getting too close to the tractor. It never got fixed, but he managed well on three legs. The dogs lived outside, not in the house. Cats were on the farm but not as pets. They were wild and lived in the barn. We fed them milk, and they were kept well fed dealing with the rats in the barn.

I used to hunt rabbits in the winter. When I was in grade eight, on New Year's Eve, I went hunting in the afternoon but didn't see any rabbits. When I hung the 22 gun on the wall, I had forgotten to remove the shell. The gun went off while my hand was covering the barrel. The bullet went through the flesh, but not the bone of my right hand, and lodged in the basement step. I never told my parents or saw a doctor. I went upstairs, put two Band-Aids on and had a sleep. That evening, we went to a neighbour's house, where we played football in the snow. I was quarterback—OUCH! By the time school was back in session, my hand was healed. I still have two scars on my hand, but the injury never really bothered me after the initial pain. I was very lucky, and because no one else knew what happened, I didn't lose use of the gun.

Horses initially played a huge role in farming, but mechanical tractors had replaced them during my youth. We had a horse named Banner who did not like to be ridden. After being bucked off more than once, I never acquired a desire to ride horses. Interesting to note that the demand for oats decreased with the decrease in the horse population.

Although we had pigs on the farm, my memory of them is vague. I do remember my father did not like them and more than once remember him losing his temper trying to load the pigs in the truck to take to market. Another memory that I wasn't allowed to forget was when I made a big mistake. I used to want to be the first person to see a new calf. The barn had many stalls for cows but also a pen for a big old sow pig. One morning, I got up early knowing there would likely be a new calf. Much to my surprise, there was a new calf, but it was in the pig pen. I rushed back to the house to tell my parents the shocking news that "the pig had given birth to a calf."

Chickens were very popular on farms because they provided a source of income selling eggs and as roasters. My father did not like chickens but Morris was allowed to have a project raising them. I remember the little chicks coming home and staying in the basement under a heat lamp for a few weeks. They were then moved to an outside building. I remember they would peck each other to death, and a substance had to be applied to their backsides to stop the pecking. I don't know if Morris made any money, but I remember not liking to work with them.

Cattle were the most important animal on our farm. We initially had milk cows and a cow-calf operation. Cows provided income from the sale of cream and also the sale of the calves. Cows had to be milked twice daily, so you were required to always be close to home. Cows have a leader in the pasture and know when to come "home" to be milked. Cows know their stall in the barn and do not mind being chained up. This didn't prevent them kicking at the person doing the milking. The cows stayed outside in the summer but in the winter spent nights in the warmth of the barn. To the best of my knowledge, we didn't sell milk or butter, only cream. The cows would be milked into pails that would be carried to the house to separate the cream from the milk. A milk separator had a handle you used to crank to get the milk spinning. When it was the right speed, a bell would ring, and the cream would be separated, put in a "cream can," and hauled to Prince Albert to sell.

We drank whole milk or milk that had not been separated. Cows would eat grass in the pasture. When I was quite young, our milk cows got into a patch of stinkweed. Consequently, our milk was contaminated. The smell and taste had such a negative impact on me that I never drank milk, other than chocolate milk, after that.

"Rowdy" taught me a couple of valuable lessons. Rowdy was a black-and-white calf that my father "gave" me. When I took the milk out to the calves, he always got more than his share. I even took $5 from my father's wallet to buy a special food supplement for him. Although not caught, my guilt for stealing caused me to confess. One day, I came home from school, and Rowdy was no more, but the freezer was full of meat. A price was paid for doing the wrong thing. Rowdy was too fat to sell, so he got butchered—at least that was what I was told.

In 1955, when I was eight, our grandparents came to live at our farm for a year. That's because where they were living was too wet for their cattle. So, they moved into our garage with their milk cows being hauled—not herded—about 60 miles to our farm, where it was sandy and much better for the cows. Neighbours helped them get from Crooked River. This included the cow that served as the herd's leader, a Holstein that Bestapa called Old Mrs. Sommerville. He always gave cows a woman's name.

They lived in the car garage, which was attached to the larger garage. Its main door was sealed and a window installed on the south side. When they arrived, the necessities to cook were added.

The space was very limited, but they insisted on keeping the cream separator there.

During that time, I don't remember them spending time in our house or us in theirs even though I loved spending time outside or in the barn with Bestapa and the milk cows and calves. After about a year, they moved back to Crooked River, and we returned the car to the garage—a garage that now had a window at the front. In the early 1960s, my father converted from milk cows to a feedlot, which ended the use of the barn, and it was replaced with a corral and a shed.

My oldest brother, Clayton, became a cattle buyer right after completing high school, a career he enjoyed all his life.

Although animals supplemented our income, grain was the major source of income. We farmed eight quarters of land, which was quite a large farm at the time. The primary crops grown were wheat, barley and oats. Rapeseed and flax were also planted, but to a much lesser degree. Rape was later replaced by canola, a similar looking plant. They both produced a cooking oil. My daughter liked seeing a yellow field and asking Dad what it was. My father never disappointed by saying, "It's rape, but people call it canola now." Fertilizers were used on some crops but not to the extent used today. Land was "summer fallowed," or not seeded, every third year.

It seemed like work was never done on the farm. Upon reflection, it also seems like I didn't do much of it. In the spring, the seed had to be prepared. This meant putting the seed through a seed cleaning machine. The seeding was always done by Dad or an older brother or farmhand. The garden had to be planted, but Mom did almost everything but the potatoes.

In the summer, hay had to be baled and stacked. My allergies saved me from this unpleasant task. The crops were sprayed, but we were just used as markers to show what had been done. It's doubtful the spray was very healthy! Summer fallow had to be cultivated a few times each summer. This job appealed to me, and I was driving a tractor at a very early age. I remember the dealer being very surprised to arrive at the field and see me driving. It had a hand clutch, and I stood while driving. I was too small to sit on the seat and drive.

In the fall, harvest included the garden as well as the crops. We all worked to bring in the vegetables from the garden. Driving the combine was always done by someone other than me. Driving the truck and hauling the grain to be stored on the farm, I enjoyed. The truck had a hoist, and the bins were now round and required little or no shovelling.

The cattle were year-round work. They had to be fed daily and cows milked twice daily. "Chop" had to be made and fed. Grain was fed into a hammer mill and crushed to make it safe to eat. Hay had to be fed and straw provided as bedding. Straw bales were made in the fall after combining, and unfortunately, I had no allergies to straw so I became a labourer! Manure had to be removed!

Straw could be baled or just worked back into the soil. Flax straw, however, would not decompose, so it had to be burned. The field would be harrowed, and each little individual pile would have to be lit. Burning the straw also burnt off our eyelashes. I think we had the longest lashes in school, because they grew in longer. Grain could only be sold when the elevators accepted deliveries. Birch Hills had six or seven elevators, though the population was less than 500. Dad hauled most of the grain to town, and the railway hauled it away. I often went for the experience and to be with Dad. In early days, there would be long lineups at the elevator, so you got to spend hours in town.

Other chores were picking rocks out of the fields, picking roots, building and repairing fences, washing equipment and vehicles, painting and repairing buildings and much, much more. It's funny how we always seem to want what we don't have. We had great home-cooked meals but dreamed of having restaurant food. Later, we dreamed of having home-cooked meals. Much of our food was gathered from the land, but store-bought groceries always seemed special.

There were two small grocery stores within four miles of the farm. Gorenson's, later Heglands, served the Winton district, and the family lived right in the store. It was on the road to get to the ferry we crossed to go to Prince Albert. Gorenson's even had a gas pump where you could see the gas in the glass container above the pump. Ryder's Grocery Store was on the route to the church, in the opposite direction of the school. We purchased very little here but knew the family. Birch Hills also had a much larger grocery store and a bakery. The bakery was a separate business, not part of the grocery store. Most items would be bought in Birch Hills, but seldom was a "treat" bought at the bakery. I remember that bread was seventeen cents per loaf. Baked goods were usually prepared at home. We also would use the butcher in Birch Hills to prepare the animal meat that we brought in—pork and beef cuts. No family member hunted, so we very seldom ate wild meat, duck, geese, deer or moose. They were hunted by neighbours but never by us.

We never had a meal without saying grace. Our breakfasts were always hearty. In the winter, it was typically oatmeal or cream of wheat, and we sometimes ate pancakes, waffles, eggs and bacon. Our noon meal was called "dinner," and our evening meal was called "supper." The noon meal was often a hot one. "Lunch" referred to a snack between meals and what we called the meal we took to school. We never, unless there were guests, drank coffee on the farm. We drank tea, which is unusual in a Norwegian home.

When asked what it was like growing up with me years after I had left the farm, Morris responded, "He kept the family in fish." It's impossible to talk about my childhood without talking about the river. Saskatchewan has two major rivers: the North Saskatchewan and the South Saskatchewan. Our farm was on the banks of the South Saskatchewan, and the North Saskatchewan ran through Prince Albert. They joined to become one at "The Forks" twenty miles east of the city.

I don't know who taught me to fish. I do know it was not my dad, because he disliked fishing. I never owned a rod and reel but fished with a throw line. You bought a green line and attached four hooks about two feet apart near the end of the line. A weight was attached to the end. You attached the other end to a stick in the ground and threw the line into the river. A willow was connected in front of the stick with some slack, and when it jerked, you had a bite. I always envied the farms that had earthworms, because the other bait was grasshoppers. It's much easier to dig for earthworms than catch grasshoppers to fill an empty Coke bottle—but I did. Grasshoppers were easier to catch early in the morning—they moved more slowly when they were damp from the dew than when the sun was hot.

Riding your bike 40 miles to return to fish at The Forks seems illogical. But fishing is always better where you are not—it's one of the nonsensical beliefs of fishermen. I did the bike ride a few times but mostly fished not too far from the farmyard. Goldeye was the edible fish caught, and many were kept in the deep freeze and often eaten. I did keep the family in fish! I don't know any other boys who spent so much time fishing alone, but the solitude and excitement were great for me.

One sad memory of fishing was one evening when I caught a fish over ten pounds. A goldeye that weighed over two pounds was considered large, so I was used to catching fish under two pounds. My parents were in Prince Albert, so I called our neighbour Jim Manson, and he came over to see what I had caught. He identified it as a sturgeon. For me, this was one huge fish! When I got up the next morning, I ran in to tell my parents—who were now home from Prince Albert—the news about my fish. In turn, they told me that Grandma Agnew had passed away the night before. I know exactly when I caught that big fish. I have a picture somewhere, and it reminds me how inconsequential an important event can become in a moment of time.

Weather has a very different perspective on the farm than in the city. Spring is an exciting time. The weather warms, the snow melts, the birds return, the trees bud and it's time to prepare for planting. Summers are very pleasant with the temperatures normally in the 70-degree (F), 21-degree (C) range. Celsius was not being used when I was on the farm. Rain was critical, and the crops were very dependent on the amount and timing. Wind was tiring, but thankfully did not blow hard very often. We would ideally get a couple of days of a slow, steady rain, and thunderstorms were also welcome. Fall delivered frequently bright sunny skies, necessary for harvesting. Temperatures cooled a bit, but the weather was pleasant unless winter approached too early. We had snow on Halloween about half of the time. Winter could bring huge snowstorms, winds and very cold temperatures. Minus 40 degrees is the same for Fahrenheit and Celsius, and we would experience it for a few days each winter. Each season had pluses and minuses, and I still enjoy the positive aspect of each season.

We never felt that we were poor—in fact, we felt we were better off than most of our neighbours. Our farm may not have been any better than the neighbours', but we were proud of it and how we maintained it. My father often said, "Nothing ever had more impact on quality of life than electricity." All the farms had electricity, so maybe we were not better off other than in our young minds.

"Yard poles" lit up thousands of farms. Refrigerators, washing machines, electric stoves, deep freezers and running water impacted the home. Outside, milking machines, welding equipment, grain dryers, drills and many other items made farm work much easier.

Other than visits to Bestamo and Bestapa's and our uncles and families in Crooked River, which was about 70 miles away, my world was very seldom more than a 30-mile radius from the farm. The exception was when I went away 200 miles (360 km) for school in grade nine. Other than a school bus, there were no bus rides, train trips or airplane travels. No time or energy was spent on the outside world. We spent a lot of time with family.

Our most frequent visitors were extended family, and few guests ever spent the night. Our visits were most likely to the homes of our relatives, not our neighbours. It is easy to be critical of living in such a "small world." But think of a world where the world's problems don't exist, sports are played rather than watched, weather is prayed about rather than fretted about and your clothes are never out of style. I don't think there could have been a better, less worrisome childhood. And don't forget the vast amount of time spent outdoors in the natural environment.

Money, then as now, was useful to have available. I never worked for anyone other than my father until after completing high school. My pay was $5/week maximum, plus room, board, clothing and other essentials plus many fun experiences. Although we were expected to work on the farm, we were not discouraged from using our resources to get some cash. Three pests on the Saskatchewan prairies were gophers, crows and magpies. The government, before my time, paid a penny for every gopher tail. The schools paid for crow and magpie legs and eggs. By the time I started school, money was no longer offered for gopher tails, but the reward for crow and magpie legs and eggs was still in practice. This never proved much value to me. Eggs were seasonal and not abundant on our property. And without a gun, it was not practical to acquire legs, but I tried.

Even though the school no longer paid for gopher tails, Dad did. I spent many hours trapping gophers on our 40-acre pasture. Traps were relatively inexpensive and lasted a long time. I don't remember making much money but felt I was improving the farm by ridding it of pests. And it also meant doing what I liked best—being alone wandering about the farm. Soon, poison became a more effective way of dealing with the gopher population.

I had an interesting trapping experience once—and that was when I was trapping gophers the day Mom gave me her watch so I would know when to come home for lunch. Her mother had given her the watch, a gold ladies watch, and she was very clear about how important it was not to lose it. I'm not really sure why she chose to give it to me. And, you know what happened. I had traps in different places in the pasture and was going from one to the other, when I realized the watch was gone. My heart sank when I realized this, especially since the pasture was mighty big! I had been taught that God answered prayers, so I decided to see what would happen if I prayed. "Lord, if you help me find the watch, I will become a missionary when I grow up." Unbelievably, I walked to a gopher hole that was some distance away—and there it was!! I quickly thanked the Lord but did leave Him with the idea that I would become a missionary only if he *really* wanted me to.

My next money-maker was taking my children's-sized bike and putting a regular-sized wheel on the front. This meant it had a small wheel on the back and a large wheel on the front. It was very unique and very much in demand for a ride at school. So, I decided to charge a fee for the privilege. This didn't last long, though, after some parent complained about their child asking for money to ride the bike. After learning about this, the teacher immediately put a stop to my entrepreneurial enterprise.

Another, and more profitable, venture was selling Kool-Aid. You could order and pay for a kit, sell the Kool-Aid packages at a markup and keep the profit. The problem for me was that homes were few and far between, and the bicycle was my delivery vehicle. I remember Bjarney asking me what happens if someone doesn't want to buy. I told him I just sighed, wiped the sweat off my forehead and usually then got a sale. He laughed, as did my dad.

Many farms had cisterns and would buy water, particularly in the winter. We had a roadway to the river, plus a truck and a 500-gallon water tank. We loaded up the water, and I delivered it to neighbours for $5. I got to keep this money if I did the work. In high school, I was given a vehicle with a full tank of gas every Saturday night and money enough to have fun.

Aerial photo of farmyard showing proximity to river

Brian, Mom, Clayton, Dad, and Morris (Murray not yet born)

Family outing in "Lemon" Oldsmobile

Mom and friends enjoying a higher view

Murray, Brian, and Morris with the garden tractor

Combines unloading grain into truck to be stored

Dad, Mom, Ernie and Gail Friesen, Bjarney Stangeland, Bestamo, Cora Stangeland

Brian, Dad, Clayton, Murray, Mom, and Morris `

3

MORE ABOUT FAMILIES

I n my youth, the father was the breadwinner, and the mother had home responsibilities. Even though there were four sons and no daughters, we were never expected to do chores in the house. We never washed clothes, washed dishes or even made our bed. We were even annoyed when we had to do the dishes on Mother's Day! And that was after not helping with cooking or setting the table.

Mom was physically a small person and a very private person. I never once remember her complaining about her workload. In hindsight, we should have been much more appreciative of all the things she did for us. She cooked, cleaned, canned, managed the garden, planted flowers, washed the clothes, acted as our nurse and much, much more. When I woke up with sore legs as a boy, she would get up and rub Watkins liniment on them. When I had a cold, she would put a mustard plaster on my chest. She did many, many things to and for us to make our lives better.

On the other hand, I do not remember Mom doing many farm chores or field work. She would, however, deliver meals to the field during seeding and harvesting times. She would play indoor games with us, but I do not recall her playing outdoor ones.

She seldom, if ever, wore makeup, and, although pretty, she disliked having her picture taken. More than once, she defaced pictures so you could not see her face. She dressed neatly but not such that she would stand out. She did wear jewellery and had fur coats. I think the coats were more for warmth than fashion.

Although Mom was quiet, she was very determined and independent. She often drove the car, something not common for women in our district. We often went to Prince Albert without Dad and crossed the ferry doing so. We never had to wonder if we were behaving poorly. We also never had to wonder if Dad was behaving poorly. I don't, however, remember Dad telling her she was behaving badly.

Religion was a very important part of Mom's life. While growing up, she always read us Bible stories. And every night, we kneeled and prayed:

Now I lay me down to sleep
I pray the Lord my soul to keep
If I should die before I wake
I pray the Lord my soul to take
Amen

She read the Bible, did daily personal devotions, regularly attended church and was involved with the women's mission group. She was very supportive but insisted we follow the strict rules of the church. This included not really approving girls that wore makeup, plus dancing, swearing, lying and cheating. We knew the importance of the Ten Commandments. We also knew we would likely be up to no good after midnight—midnight curfews were very, very annoying to me. She never spoke badly of other people, and I never knew anyone to speak badly of her.

Although she never spanked us and seldom even shouted at us; I do remember her chasing us out of the house with a broom. I don't remember our Agnew grandparents ever visiting the farm, and they never spoke of the past. As previously mentioned, we didn't even know they had been successful farmers in Winton. I do remember frequent visits to them in Prince Albert, and Morris and I staying over. Gramma didn't like us playing with the boys across the street, because they were not well supervised or well behaved. I guess, in her mind, we were!

Grandpa Agnew smoked a pipe and liked to walk downtown with us. We would just sit and watch people, an exercise I continued my entire life—watching people. One day, Morris and I set out on our own, and a dog attacked him but not me; a very scary outing, more for Morris than for me! I don't remember our conversations with them but do remember Grandpa taking a nip of brandy out of the cupboard before bed. We hoped Mom didn't catch him! Grandma Agnew passed away in 1958 and Grandpa not long after in 1960.

Dad was the opposite of Mom in that she needed to be alone to re-energize, and he needed to be around people to do so. I went to neither funeral. He was not afraid of work and expected his sons to work to improve our farm—not to be working for others. Having to leave home as a very young person and with only a grade five education, hard work and ambition resulted in us having a farm with over 1,000 acres and the equipment necessary to farm it. He was very independent and not afraid to take risks—farming is a high-risk business. There is no doubt his ambition influenced my decision to independently prove myself.

Dad had a very quick temper that luckily was usually directed at animals and things—not his sons. He would be over-the-top mad, and fifteen minutes later be entirely over what had made him mad. His father had a very unusual sense of humour that he inherited, as did I and other relatives. Humour can be very effective in curbing anger. Dad was loyal to his family and helped them whenever possible. He was also a loyal church goer and a lifetime supporter of the church. He was proud of his accomplishments and very responsible with his money unless he was buying a watch or a new car. I too have spent more than necessary to own these items. It's strange how many ways our parents have influenced our behaviour.

One of his most memorable quotes was, "People have told me it was too bad to be born at a time of no opportunity." He heard it as a child, a parent, a grandparent and a great-grandparent. He concluded it was true for some people, and for others they had to choose which opportunity to pursue. Attitude matters! I also remember the day when, after lunch, he lay down for a nap and sent me out in the heat and wind to drive the tractor. I asked why he got to nap and not me. He replied, "When you are old and work, you get tired, and when you are young and work, you get in shape." I don't think driving the tractor gets you in shape, but I got the message.

We visited with Dad's relatives much more than the Agnews. After 90 years in Canada, the Hesje family has annual gatherings that attract up to 80 people. There has been an annual gathering before Christmas that includes a curling bonspiel, a crokinole tournament, dinner, songs and the Christmas story. We have also had large family celebrations at the farm. A horseshoe tournament is always popular. The birthday party for Dad's 80th was one such event.

My parents never fought or even had angry arguments in front of us. They never struck each other or spanked any of we boys. At least not me. Neither of them smoked or drank alcohol. Dad always laughed about Gordon Phillips, a neighbour, telling him, "I feel sorry for you because when you wake up, you know it's the best you will feel all day." I am not sure a hangover is worth knowing you will feel better later in the day.

As loving a family as my parents were, I never saw them kiss, and we were not a hugging family. I am still not a hugger. I don't remember telling each other we loved them. Emotions were not expressed, but actions were monitored. We were not encouraged to express our feelings and never did. Crying was for sissies, not farm boys.

My mother passed away twenty years before my father, and he often said, "I have no bad memories of your mom or being with her." When I challenged him, his answer was, "I have forgotten all the bad memories so only have good ones left." Something we all should do more often.

Clayton, my oldest brother, was seven years older than me. I have very few memories of him living at home. He finished high school away from home. He was married at age 21, the same age as his dad, and he and his wife Bev had a son, Brent, before I finished high school. We were always proud of our oldest brother.

Morris was three years older than me. We spent much more time together and would have shared a bed when young. He was usually supportive of me but not when I had bad dreams. I remember having a recurring dream where a bear was chasing me. I would wake up scared and head for parent security. One night, the bear chased me over a cliff. I rolled out of bed and hit the floor. That was the last time I had the dream. We both were relieved. Dreams have always fascinated me, but I seldom have found any significant meaning in them.

Although we had many fun times together, it wasn't fun for him to have to take me along on Saturday night when we were in high school. He would take me, drop me off, and pick me up to go home. That worked fine until one night the restaurant closed at midnight, and he was nowhere to be seen. Much later he showed up with me standing outside under a streetlight with nobody around. When we got home, Dad was up and asked why we were so late. Morris replied, "I couldn't find Brian." I did serve a purpose, after all. Today, Morris owns the farm home quarter. He is my only brother who has any artistic talent. He has made wood carvings that could easily be sold commercially.

Murray was four years younger than me. We too shared a bed when Morris got his own room. We played together lots but had different friends at school. Murray went on to have an international career. It has always been a mystery to us that we both pursued an accounting designation. We became much closer as we aged.

We were a family that gave each other nicknames. My mom we called "Wild Thing" after the song. She was anything but wild. One day Dad called himself "Jake the Snake" and forever became the "Snake." Clayton was self-named the "Loike from Alberkoike." Morris was the "Boar" and Murray the "Toad." Unfortunately, my nickname slips my mind.

One of the best messages us boys had, at least for me, was a wall hanging in the bedroom that said, "Don't Worry It May Never Happen." Great advice if you can do it. Advice I had to remind myself of many, many times.

Hesje family gathering

Bestapa with his chickens

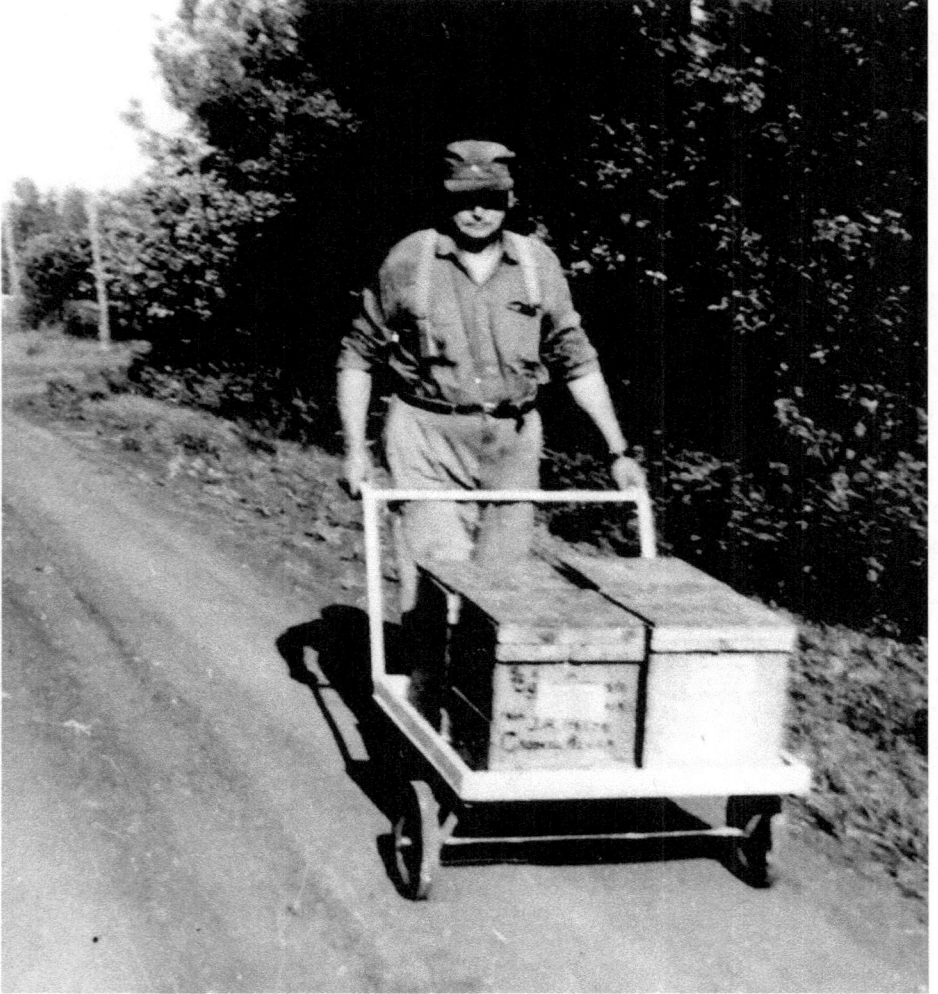

Bestepa delivering eggs to Crooked River

Bestamo making krumkake

Old Mrs. Sommerville, the lead milk cow

Morris loving his chickens

Community snow plow

Snow was fun for children but work for adults

Murray, Dad, Brian, and Clarence Hagan carding wool

Ten combines purchased; Dad is wearing the red shirt

Birch Hills Main Street

4

WHAT WE DIDN'T HAVE

We had everything we needed on the farm, but I would like to share a few things we didn't have. We didn't have computers or the Internet. Blackboards, not computer screens, were in the classroom. We never had drugs or even heard of marijuana. Law enforcement had no impaired driving laws to enforce. We had few paved roads. Roads were either gravel or mud. More were mud than gravel.

We didn't have "foreign" cars. Ford, General Motors and Chrysler were the only brands. You could tell the difference by the style rather than the emblem. The first car that I remember was an early 1950s Oldsmobile that, although it was nice, broke down often. In my memory, it seemed to break down every trip. We then switched to Plymouth and had one with a push button transmission rather than a gear shift.

We didn't have plastic bags. Groceries were purchased in paper bags. It's interesting the logic used to eliminate paper bags was to save trees. Packaging was not nearly as robust or wasteful as it is today. Lawsuits and government regulations have resulted, in my opinion, in excessive and wasteful packaging of goods. We never had helmets when riding bikes and never heard of car seats or seat belts. And we lived to tell our story.

We never had online shopping but had mail order catalogues. Eatons and Sears catalogues sold almost everything you needed. They also served as fashion information and offered many opportunities to dream about many things you would never own. They also served many outhouses with toilet paper. They were not ideal but worked and cost nothing. We never had credit cards. Cash or cheque were the forms of payment. Cash was used for the majority of transactions, because credit was not nearly as available as it is today.

We never had telephones that could be removed from the wall. Our phone was on the kitchen wall, and our number was two long and three short rings. We never had private calls, because neighbours could listen to your calls. Not great if you were refused a date with snoopy neighbours hearing. We never carried something that we were constantly having to check for messages. A benefit we never appreciated at the time. We never had cans—soda and beer were only sold in bottles. There were, of course, many other things we didn't have, but these are a few examples.

5

SCHOOL DAYS, SCHOOL DAYS

When Saskatchewan was surveyed, the land was divided into townships. A township is a square six miles long and six miles wide that contains 36 sections, each containing 640 acres. The sections are then divided into quarters containing 160 acres, the size of a homestead.

The importance the founding fathers placed on education is evident by the government allocating two sections in each township for schools. No student could be more than four miles from a school. There were over 5,000 school districts in Saskatchewan with a population less than a million. Our farm was three miles from the school.

We lived in the Winton School District, which was formed in 1909 for grades one to eight. In 1949, a new schoolhouse was built a half mile further west. My mother and oldest brother would have gone to the first school and I to the new school. I can think of at least eighteen families served by the one-room school; an indication of how small farms were at the time. There were at least six families other than ours in the district with four or more children.

The school grounds had a teacherage for the teacher, a barn for horses used to get to school, a ball diamond, swings and a large yard to play dodgeball, soccer and other games. I don't recall having a backstop for softball or nets for soccer. A homer was over the fielder's head, not the fence. Sticks of wood served as goal posts.

I don't remember ever walking the three miles to school. I vaguely remember riding in a sleigh pulled by a horse. It was winter, and we were kept warm with blankets. We usually rode our bikes, except in the winter. We were often driven to school but not always picked up. Walking home past Dad in the field, he waved, but we were mad and didn't wave back. Rather than get mad, he found it funny.

School was from September to June with holidays for Christmas and Easter. The hours were from 9:00 a.m. to 3:30 p.m. with recess morning and afternoon and a lunch break. We played outside during breaks unless it was cold or raining.

The teacher's desk was at the front of the room, and everyone knew there was a strap in one of the drawers. When you entered the school, there was a cloakroom for coats and boots. It was also where the strap was delivered—but not to me. Desks were in rows with different sizes for different grades. All my teachers were women and devoted more time to the lower grades. As you advanced, you helped younger students. In grade eight, for example, you might help grade four. The system may have had disadvantages, but you certainly learned to work on your own.

Our subjects were reading, printing and writing, arithmetic, science, social studies, health, art and music. Our grades would be

A, B, C, D, F or satisfactory or unsatisfactory. I don't remember having physical education. We got plenty of exercise without it. The measurement system we learned was the Imperial System created through the British Weights and Measurements Act of 1824 and refined over the years. In 1970, Canada converted to the metric system. When that happened, inches, feet and yards became millimetres, centimetres and metres. Fahrenheit temperatures became Celsius. Since the United States of America, our largest trading partner, didn't change, it never made sense to me that Canada did.

When I started grade one, kindergarten didn't exist. There were twenty students or more in our one-room school with all eight grades in the same room. The grade one reader was called *Dick and Jane* and included Baby Sally, a dog named Spot and a cat named Puff.

In addition to the other subjects, we had a public speaking competition. I recited the poem, "Under A Toadstool." I won the right to represent our school at the next level but lost because I had my hands in my pockets. If they had let me go to the bathroom, who knows where I would have gone with public speaking.

In grade two, I missed a few weeks of school with either measles or the chicken pox. I remember dreading going back to school, because the teacher was very strict and often yelled. I can still hear her say how happy they were to have me back. Unnecessary worry on my part!

The teachers had us place our hands on the desks in the morning to check if our hands and nails were clean. A health nurse visited the school for checkups and to give vaccinations. The smallpox vaccination was done by a quick series of pricks with a needle. It left a scar, a badge of honour. We also got a polio vaccine. No one protested or refused to have the vaccinations. The nurse also checked our eyes, and one could get a glasses prescription if needed. Seeing the dentist was the responsibility of the parents.

We took lunch to school in a lunch kit or a backpack. Backpacks were great for the bicycle. Lunch might include hot soup in a thermos, sandwiches—peanut butter and jam, and cheese were my favorites—and a treat, usually a cookie or a piece of fruit.

Every morning, the Union Jack flag was raised, and every afternoon, it was taken down and folded. The students, myself included, did this task. The current Canadian flag was adopted in 1965, the year after I left high school. Every morning, we sang "God Save the Queen," which was the National Anthem at the time. "Oh Canada" was adopted as the National Anthem in 1980.

The school and family homes would be used to raise funds for various purposes. I especially remember a bingo held at the school with parents and children. The prize I wanted to win was a knife. The prize I did win was a complete set of dishes—the grand prize. Just what a boy didn't want! We would also have box lunch socials. Moms and girls would prepare lunches in decorative boxes, which were auctioned to the men and boys. You didn't know who had made the lunch you purchased. Needless to say, there were some disappointed males and females sharing a lunch. But there were also many more happy ones!

Every year at Christmas, the school had a Christmas concert at the community hall. Every student sang, danced, was in a play or did something unusual. The hall was a quarter mile from the school, and the older students went over to light the fire so we could practice. The many practices were during school hours, so we were all more than willing to not have regular classes. The concert played to a full house.

Children's Day was an annual event that we looked forward to every spring. All the district schools would go to Birch Hills to compete in sporting events. The day began with a parade down Main Street. Each school selected colours, and all the students would be dressed in those colours. Our parents made the clothes. I remember one year, our colours were green slacks and a white top. The parade ended at the fairgrounds, where the sporting events were held. No prizes were awarded for the parade.

Participation in the sports was not optional. I competed in the foot race, high jump, broad jump, hop-step-jump and the javelin, and I believe the ball throw and discus. We practiced at our local school for days before the event. The first, second and third participants were awarded red, blue or white ribbons.

My only ribbon won was the javelin, and it was controversial. The javelin was thrown three times by each participant and had to stick when it landed in order to count. Only Bob successfully had the javelin stick in the ground. He had thrown it 128 feet. I got myself positioned to be the very last throw and just reached over the line and stuck it in the ground. Bob had thrown it over 120 feet, and his stuck. My two feet was a legitimate second but not well received by all. After much discussion, I was awarded my blue ribbon. Creativity should have its rewards.

Individual schools would travel to another school in the area to compete. The competition would always be a softball game. These games were more about fun than winning. Not so for the ball tournament that ended Children's Day. Teams played to win. Birch Hills, the town, had a much larger school and usually won. Winton School had boys and girls on their team because of our size. Winton won with both the senior and junior team between 1954–1956. My name is on the roster, but I don't remember playing for the junior team. I do remember finishing a close second in my eighth grade. I was the pitcher and was amazed we made it to the final and very disappointed when we lost in the final. A real character builder!

When I reached grade eight, there were only three students left from grade one: Mae Phillips, Carol Blanchard and myself. I don't know about their marks, but I do remember our art class. We were asked to draw a horse. Mae drew one that looked like a horse. I drew one that looked like a bunch of toothpicks randomly arranged. Embarrassing, indeed!

Other than having sleepovers at relatives' and friends' houses, I had never been away from home prior to going away for grade nine. Briercrest Bible Institute opened in October 1935, and in 1946, they purchased the Royal Crown Airforce Station Caron. It was over 350 km away from home. Many students from our church attended this school before me, including both of my older brothers.

There is no junior high for grades seven to nine. Consequently, your adjustment to high school is more of an adjustment than in other jurisdictions.

Less than a month before my 14th birthday, I was driven to my new home for the next school year. I had a nice roommate named Ed Jordan, but we never had any contact after the school year. I disliked dormitory life, communal showers and little time alone. I also disliked too many rules. The security of family and home life was gone, and I could only leave campus seven weekends during the entire year.

Every student had to do eight hours of "gratis" a week. My duties included washing dishes most of the time. A machine was used, and many students were on each shift—it could actually be fun. One day, Ed and I were given the task of sweeping out the hanger. I remember Ed saying, "Didn't your dad tell you that 'A job worth doing is worth doing well'?" He hadn't, but Dad's actions had more impact on me than his dad's words on him. We found and took some pickles and canned goods. After eating them, we got sick, and I was convinced God punished us for stealing.

I played my first organized hockey game there. I knew how to skate and had played hockey on the river but never in a rink with a referee. I broke my stick and got a penalty for not dropping the stick immediately. I didn't know the rules, was embarrassed and never played another organized hockey game in my life.

Religion played an important role in your education. The school would have three-day conferences where parents and friends attended, and services were held all day. A large thermometer was at the front stage where the preacher stood. It showed the donation goal, and a red line indicated how close donations were to reaching the goal. On a dare, I filled out an anonymous pledge card for a significant amount. The thermometer had a big gain that afternoon. I never got caught but felt bad about the prank.

Communism was a global threat at this time, and the church preached that the Communists would destroy Christians. The first Monday of every month, classes were cancelled, and we spent the day listening to student testimonials. One day, a young man with red hair got in line for his turn to give his testimony. When he got to the microphone, he testified that he had been sent by the Communist Party to gather information and names. I honestly thought he would pull out a gun and fire. The fear of Communism was that real to me. I don't know what happened to the guy, but I hope he was held accountable for the fear he caused me and others.

Newspapers and radios were not allowed. I always thought stupid rules were made to be broken, and I had a rocket-shaped crystal radio with earplugs. I hid the radio in my mattress. The rooms were often searched for contraband, but my radio was never discovered. I listened to it at night, so I had a link to the outside world in spite of all the rules.

Dating was not encouraged and carefully controlled. A service station with a restaurant was within walking distance of the school. Students could go for a hamburger, fries and a shake or whatever— the catch was that boys went on Tuesday, Thursday and Saturday, and the girls went Monday, Wednesday and Friday. I never dated at Caronport, so it bothered me less than others.

The school had good teachers, and study time in the room at night was mandatory. My marks were the best by far of my four years of high school. High marks also got you an exemption from final exams, so I got to go home early. I was relieved and happy to leave and return to fishing and the farm without all the rules.

Fortunately for me, my older brother Morris had a greater dislike for rules than me. He, after two years, received a letter from Caronport asking him not to come back. After one year at a Lutheran School in Outlook, Saskatchewan, he got the same letter. The result was that he and I were going to be headed to Birch Hills High School. I couldn't have been happier.

Birch Hills was seventeen miles from the farm, and our bus ride was much farther. We were the first to be picked up and last to be dropped off. As often as possible, we would look for an excuse for Morris or me, after getting a licence, to drive our car or truck to school. Staying after school to curl would be one example of a valid reason not to take the bus.

School was even better when I discovered two of my best friends like at Winton were now attending Birch Hills. We picked up where we had left off and remained friends during high school and after. In Saskatchewan, high school was grades nine through twelve, and grades one through eight were elementary grades. I had a teacher for each subject rather than one teacher for the whole school at Winton. Most of the teachers were men, but our French teacher was a woman. She couldn't speak French herself, so we learned how to translate but not speak Canada's second official language.

She smoked, and our nickname for her had the word "nicotine" in it.

My lack of mechanical skill was demonstrated at my first shop class at the shop. I was hammering a nail with both hands on the hammer. When the teacher made fun of me, I dropped the hammer—and the class. Instead, I became the only male student in typing for the next three years; a much better program in many ways and proved more useful when writing term papers for class.

I was never interested in running for school president or even room rep. I didn't volunteer for any committees, such as the yearbook one. The boys' soccer team, softball team and curling were the only sports I played. At my one and only football game, the coach, who wasn't fond of me, had me on the defensive line. After one crushing tackle from a much, much bigger person, my football career ended with my throwing my helmet on the ground and walking off the field for good.

Sports for me were more for the field trips than interest in the actual sport—except curling. It was to become a part of my life for years. The only other field trip we took was to the Legislature Buildings in the capital city of Regina. No exotic field trips in those days.

Every day at noon, we would walk downtown to the Union Cafe owned by the Mah family. Attractions included a great hot hamburger sandwich, a pinball machine and the fact that he would sell cigarettes for 47 cents—to a minor! One was also able to master the pinball machine and hang out with friends at the cafe.

How serious school was to me is reflected in my behaviour one fall. It was not uncommon for students to miss school to help with the harvest at home. When I was in grade XI, my friend who had a car was waiting in his car when the bus arrived at the school. He had the freedom to not take the bus, because he owned a car. He motioned me over, and we took off and spent the day relaxing in the sun and discussing our future plans. At 3:30 p.m., I was back and caught the bus home. It was a good thing until we got greedy. One afternoon, when I got off the bus at home, Dad was there to greet me. The principal had called to ask when we were going to finish harvest. No harm done, just a nice little break. No punishment! I think Dad was more concerned the principal thought he was a bad farmer than about my missing school.

We had talked about our future plans during that break. My friend Colin was hoping to take over the farm, get married and never move. My plans were for the farm to see my tail lights as soon as possible. We both pursued our different dreams.

Friends and dating were much greater priorities than marks for me. I never did much studying but knew the marks required in grade twelve to be admitted to university. The admittance requirements at that time were either 60 percent or 65 percent in the provincial departmental exams.

In June, for two weeks, I skipped school and studied for those exams at home. Breaks would include going out to the pasture to shoot gophers. The studying must have been effective, because my marks were easily high enough for university admittance.

We never had much career counselling at school. In guidance class, the principal distributed a list of occupations and earnings. Dentists were at the top of the list. It didn't take me long to decide that dentistry was for me! I was very fortunate to be in one of the first years when more students were going to university. My two older brothers didn't go, but my younger brother also got a university degree. Many of my graduating class would never have moved more than 50 miles from home after completing high school.

One of the most memorable days at school was the day it was announced over the intercom that President John F. Kennedy had been assassinated. The room went completely silent, and every student was completely stunned. A day when I and millions more remember exactly where they were when they heard the news.

In my twelve years of school, I never witnessed a fight, nor bullying. There were no protests. There was more focus on responsibility than rights. I am sure there would have been gay students, but none were openly so. It was a safe, fun environment for me. I left thinking that had I studied, I would have been at the top of the class. A belief later to prove to be untrue!

Winton Elementary School for grades first through eighth

Winton Elementary School today with the community hall in the background

Ninth grade high school at Briercrest Seminary

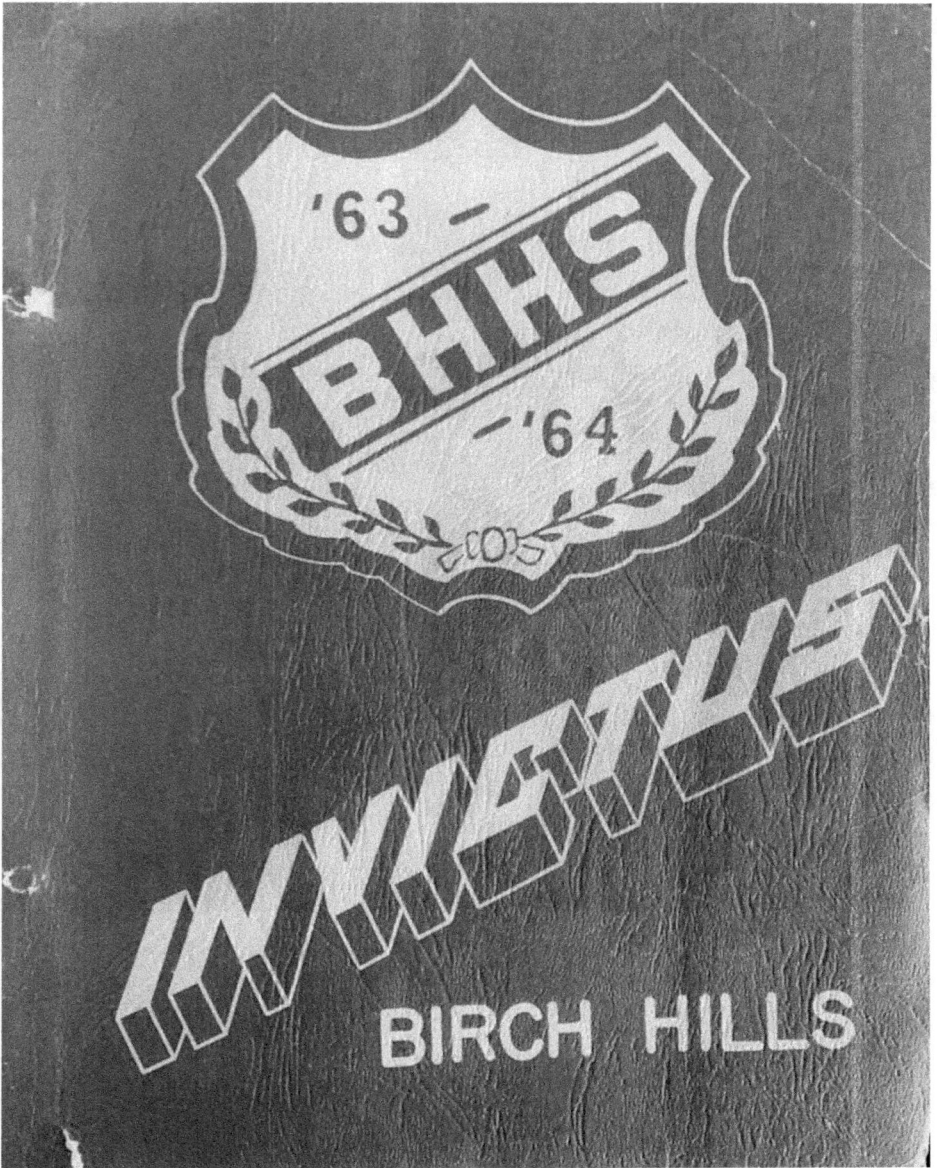

Twelfth grade yearbook for Birch Hills High School

Curling team: Bill McGillvery (lead), Bev Pushie (second), Brian Hesje (third),
Grant Hastings (skip)

Soccer

BACK ROW: L to R - Allen Thoen, Barry Stangland, Billy MacGilvary, Jim Gordon, Richard Belamy, Donald Yeaman, Ralph Brewster, Sheldon Getz, Brian Hesji, Mr. Derkach (coach)

Brian, wearing a striped sweater, was an outstanding goalie

Boy's Softball

BACK ROW: L to R - Allan Michell, George Joyes, Denny Foster,
   Kelly Strand, Terry Welch, Coach-Mr. Shultz.
SECOND ROW: L to R - Brian Hesje, Dwight Meyers, Milton Birk-
   land, Les Thompson, Terry Hegland.
KNEELING: L to R - Barry Stangeland, Bill Demerais.

Brian, wearing a school jacket, was an all-star third baseman

6

FUN DURING FARM YEARS

The way we entertained ourselves on the farm may seem old-fashioned today, but many of the things we did are still being done today. One thing is I think we were given more opportunity to use our imagination. Not that we had bigger imaginations, but we were not registered in a multitude of activities. There was no organized hockey, soccer, swimming, skiing, music or one of the other many activities that parents register their children in today.

But we did have plenty of fun. We loved to play ball, but because our school had so few students, boys and girls played the same sports. We played softball, not baseball. At home, we had to be more creative with only two or three players.

If there were two players, the batter would stand at the house and hit the ball at the garage. If the fielder caught the ball before it hit the garage, it was an out. Three outs, and you switched positions. If the ball hit the garage, it was a single, the big door a double, the car garage door a triple and the small window at the attic a home run. I only remember one home run—it broke the window. Dad replaced it with a wooden board.

When we had three players, we used the garage as a backstop and had a batter, pitcher and catcher. A great hit could hit the house. As luck would have it, the day Clayton's future in-laws came to meet our parents, we hit the ball through the living room window and bounced it off the television into the living room. Great first impressions!

Getting a new softball was huge. One day, Dad came home with a new ball and decided to show us how far he could "throw it." He put it in an old nylon stocking Mom no longer used and twirled it round and round. The nylon wasn't strong enough, and the ball went through the sock, high and far. Right into the middle of the river. Our new ball was gone.

Since Dad's cousins, the Stangelands, had eight children, we would at times have a more typical game in their cow pasture. Just two families of parents and kids having a great time. The river was a great opportunity for fun. We often swam in the river unsupervised. No swimming lessons for us, but self-learned dog paddle experts. Sometimes during haying or harvesting, Dad and a neighbour would join us for an evening swim. Bathing suits were not necessary. In the winter, we played hockey, and I spent many, many hours fishing. The river created countless hours of enjoyment.

A memorable day was when Murray and I and a cousin went swimming. His mother had told him not to go in the river unsupervised, but we persuaded him to join us. Our clothes were on three separate rocks with his clothes in the middle. While we were in the water, a little whirlwind picked up his clothes and flung them in the water. We thought God had sent him a clear message!

I remember going to at least one rodeo. The star was a bull named Zero—he bucked off every cowboy. We rode calves when we were small but never got good enough to consider being in the rodeo. When we got a corral, we would practice walking the rails in the winter when you could fall and not get dirty. In spring, we would have friends down to try their luck. They would always fall, and almost always into the wet manure on the inside. Our practice saved us.

Christmas was always a special time. We would spend hours searching the catalogues and imagining owning new bikes, games, clothes and other toys. I remember spending Christmas Eve at the Hesje grandparents. We always opened gifts on Christmas Eve. Strangely, I only remember woolen socks as a gift. I guess dreaming of things was more important than getting them.

The church had a concert every year, and I was a participant but not a star. I remember being told to move my lips but not sing. Similar advice to that received at school. I would like to think I should have been one of the wise men but don't recall having that role.

Birthdays were also special. Every year, Mom made each of us our favourite cake—mine was angel food. She would wrap coins in wax paper and put them in the cake before icing it. Finders were keepers. One year, I remember gathering around the radio waiting for birthday greetings. The announcer wished me "Happy

Birthday" and said my gift was under the bed in the guest room. Strange, but I remember the experience, not the gift.

I don't remember cooking but do remember making pull taffy. It was fun slathering our hands with butter and pulling the toffee until it was gold coloured and then making it into braids. One night when we were home alone, Morris and I made toffee and got distracted. The toffee burned so badly in the pan that we couldn't scrape the pan clean. We threw it over the riverbank. I wonder if Mom ever missed the pan.

An unusual form of fun, and one Mom disliked, was "rubbering" on the phone. A number of families were on the same line, so you could listen in on your neighbours' calls without them knowing. It could be boring, but more often proved to be quite entertaining.

We played many of the games still played today. There was Hide and Seek, Monopoly, Scrabble, Clue, Checkers and Chinese Checkers. We also played Ping Pong or Table Tennis. We played it on the dining room table, because there wasn't room for an official size table. My father had traded a wagon with rubber wheels for the dining room set. It still sits proudly at the farm.

When the school got an official table, my brother and I were the best players. We were finalists in a school competition and played one game each day for three days. I lost the first day but won the next two. I probably would have forgotten had I lost.

Although card games weren't allowed because of our church beliefs, we played a card game called Rook. It is a card game where the ace is replaced by a one. Other replacements are Jack (eleven), Queen (twelve), King (thirteen), plus a fourteen card. The deck has

56 cards, not 52. Rather than suits of hearts, diamonds, spades and clubs, cards are coloured red, blue, green and black. The game involves taking tricks much like the game of rummy. The other card game we played was Old Maid.

The games that demonstrated my competitiveness are crokinole and horseshoes. Crokinole is played on a round wooden board with a hole in the centre surrounded by eight pegs. You shoot black or white wooden discs with your finger at the centre hole for a twenty score or to knock your opposition's disc off the playing surface. Almost every prairie farm would have had such a board. I loved the game and spent countless hours practicing on my own.

Horseshoes is an outdoor game with two to four players using four horseshoes and two targets 40 feet apart. Points are scored by landing closest to the stake or getting a "ringer." The first team or person to get 21 points wins. One day, Dad, who never "let" you win, came in for lunch and I suggested we have a game. I had practiced for hours by myself. I threw seven ringers in a row, beating him 21 to zero. I didn't play him for quite a while after that now that I had avenged all my previous losses. Years later, I won a horseshoe tournament at the lake three years in a row.

In 1956, I joined our local 4H Grain Club. I was only ten and the youngest member. Dad seeded a two-acre parcel for my brother and one for me. The plots were near home, and Gateway barley was the crop. The plot had a four-foot border that had to be kept free of weeds and a sign made for the plot. When the crop was harvested, you took a sample to a final exhibit where you also wrote an exam. I spent much time picking weeds, selecting seeds for my sample and studying for the exam. The grain samples and exam were at the school one weekend in the fall. I remember playing outside while they were marking the exams and got hit in the face by a mud lump. It hurt until the leader told me I had won.

Every summer, the Exhibition or fair would come to Prince Albert. I never liked the rides other than the crash cars. I did like throwing darts and trying to win a teddy bear and the cotton candy and caramel apples. Grandpa Agnew used to sneak us into the grounds rather than pay. We certainly never told Mom.

As a teenager, Saturday nights were spent in town. We regularly would attend the movies at the Dreamland Theatre. We occasionally would go five pin bowling in Prince Albert and sometimes even to a drive-in movie. But most of the time, we just drove around listening to music on the radio and spending time with friends.

In younger years, at Halloween, we seldom went to neighbours to trick and treat, and if we did, it was only to a few farms. But our school would make a "House of Horror" in the basement. The older students did the preparations, and the younger students got to attend. The best trick was to peel grapes and put them in a dish. When the blindfolded children felt them in the dark, they were "cat's eyeballs."

As we got older, we would trick rather than treat. I remember one year when Murray and a friend "soaped" the tractors at a neighbour's farm. One of our tractors was in the yard, and it was not soaped. Smart detective work was not necessary to pin the deed on Murray. Power in farmyards was controlled from a pole in the yard that also had a yard light. We would sneak up and pull the switch, and the power in the house would go off. One year, we poured syrup on my uncle's front step and then shut the power off. My uncle came out in his wool socks and was immediately glued to the steps. Another time, a neighbour came out and fired his shotgun into the air. We were hiding in a stack of bales, but I still remember my legs shaking at the time.

Television was not taken for granted as it is today. Television was new and very, very exciting. My earliest memory of watching television was at the home of the Short family. They lived four miles from us, and their family was older than we were. They allowed us to come over on Saturday night to watch *Stampede Wrestling*. My favourite wrestlers were Whipper Billy Watson and Little Beaver—a 4-foot, 4-inch midget whose real name was Lionel Girouc.

I remember the day when we got our first television. I was not feeling well and had spent the day in bed. A crew came late in the afternoon to install a 50-foot antenna on our roof. We lived in the river valley, and the television station had opened in Saskatoon, over a hundred miles away, in 1954. Lying in bed, I still remember all the noise they made on the roof. But it was a very big day!

When Prince Albert got a CBC station in January of 1958, our reception was much better. The televisions were all in black and white, and the screen could be snowy and unclear. Programs were not 24 hours a day with much of the late night and morning just showing an Indian-head test pattern. Every night, the station would sign off with the national anthem, "God Save The Queen."

Favorite programs included *I Love Lucy, Hockey Night in Canada, Perry Mason with Raymond Burr* and *Alfred Hitchcock Presents*. We got to know the names of hockey and baseball players such as Jean Beleveau and Mickey Mantle. The World Series was a favorite. *The Ed Sullivan Show* was a favourite show on Sunday night. I remember September 9, 1956, because our parents let us go to a neighbour's to watch the appearance of Elvis Presley for the first time. They only showed Elvis from the waist up, so we wouldn't see his gyrating legs. Another favourite was The Rifleman with Chuck Conners. One night, our parents were in Prince Albert, and my younger brother and I were home. I, for reasons unknown, jumped on the couch with the BB gun in hand and became the Rifleman. Unfortunately, I shot and shattered the protective glass on the television, rather than the bad guy. Weeks later, when our father noticed that the glass was gone, the consequences were minimal.

Birch Hills opened a curling rink when I started attending high school. I loved the game and played as often as possible. You could go to competitions called bonspiels almost every weekend. We won Brylcreem hair cream as our prize three weeks in a row. I took a tube and ran a long, white stripe down the road for laughs. Our days were often fun-filled and stress free. As you can tell from my memories, my wins are much more evident than my losses. Rest assured I also learned how to lose!

7

THEN THERE WAS CHURCH

Next to the school, the church was the greatest outside influence on our family. We attended the Lake Park Baptist Church. The church, only a few miles from the farm, was founded in 1909. It is very likely Dad attended the church as a boy, because it was in the district where his family immigrated. I still find it hard to believe that I thought for decades my mother, not my father, was the reason we attended this church.

Every Sunday, we got dressed up—Dad in a suit, Mom in a nice dress and we boys in our "Sunday Best." The attendance was usually between 40 and 60 people. Fewer than twenty families were represented, and none were families from school.

Baptists always have very upbeat music, so I enjoyed the music even though I have no musical talent. The Sunday School classes were separated by age from preschool to young people to adult and in between. I advanced from "beginner" to "young people."

In my Aunt Ruth's book, *The Way We Were*, about the Hesje family, she wrote about her parents' priorities. They were love of God, the church, their children, their neighbours and each other—

not necessarily in that order. Material things were far down the list. Work hard, be reliable, don't drink, smoke, dance or play cards. And, above all, keep the laws of the land. These were the rules to live by. My parents also believed in those teachings, but I must admit to experimenting with some of the "do not's."

I didn't particularly like going to Daily Vacation Bible School during summer holidays. No privacy, and I missed a whole week of fishing! I didn't like some of the activities but always liked competition. I won the memorize the most Bible verses competition. I thought the prize was a knife, and it was a wall hanging with a verse that glowed in the dark. My parents were displeased with how I handled my disappointment.

We never worked on Sunday, even during harvest. I remember combining until midnight Saturday and starting again on Sunday at midnight. My father insisted those that worked Sunday broke a commandment and didn't finish any earlier. He said they had more breakdowns because of fatigue. Facts seemed to indicate we finished as early as anybody.

Money was not discussed in our house, because it was the root of all evil. Not money itself but the love of money. Having a love of money, as I understand it, was breaking the word of God to have no other gods before him. These teachings have very much influenced me in that I do not believe that possessions define success. Mom disliked going to church after we bought a new car. That's because Dad wanted to show it off, and Mom disliked any time someone showed off, especially if it was her husband or one of her children.

Speaking of money, I remember our pastor came to visit and talked to Dad about the importance of tithing. He emphasized it should be ten percent of gross, not net, income. Even I knew no farmer could afford to do that. When the pastor finished, my dad said, "I think the Lord would prefer if I gave a little less so I can give again next year."

Mom and Dad went to evening service much more than us boys. We seldom attended Wednesday prayer meetings, either. I would attend Friday night Young People events. More because I could get the car than the truck if I went to church events.

A defining moment for me was one Friday night when I was in grade ten. After school, a girl asked me to help her carry a turkey to her home. As we were walking, she asked if I was going to the teen dance that night. I said yes. When my parents found out it was a dance, they wouldn't drive me into town. The girl ended up being my first date, but this was not forgiven by me for a very long time.

The strict rules of the church with no opportunity to discuss them resulted in my having a negative attitude towards church when I finished high school. I felt the rules meant my parents didn't trust me! Having said that, the teachings of the church have been much more beneficial than harmful to me on life's journey.

Lake Park Baptist Church (then)

Lake Park Baptist Church (now); the Church has thrived

8

REFLECTIONS

Life on the farm shaped me in countless ways; some I'm aware of, and others I'm just starting to realize. And I'm sure it shaped me in numerous ways I will never realize. When I go back to the farm today, over 70 years later, much is the same. The house and garage, the two most dominant features, are still present. The house has been refinished, but the structure is the same. The garage has hardly changed. The fields still grow similar crops. The river still flows, and the rapids can still be heard. One difference is that the little tree Mom planted near the house is now a big tree near the house. A tribute to her many contributions.

When I go to Birch Hills today, much has changed. The Saskatchewan Wheat Pool where we sold our grain is gone, as is the CN Railroad that carried the grain to market. All the elevators are gone! Also gone are the hospital, which is now a senior's home, the Dreamland Theatre, the Massey Harris and Case implement dealers, the car dealerships, the pool hall and barber shop, the jewellery store, the bakery, the Canadian Imperial Bank of Commerce and the grocery and hardware stores of my era.

The grocery and hardware stores are replaced by a new, large co-op store, but most of the businesses have just disappeared. There are many new houses and a four-story condominium building. The school remains and appears to be well maintained. The ice arena and curling rink are still well used. The ice arena is now called the Hesje Centre, since our family funded some much-needed maintenance. The golf course has been much improved, as are the fairgrounds, and a small airport now exists.

Although the town has grown to over 1,000 people, it is more likely because of its proximity to Prince Albert than services provided. Unbelievably, the hotel is still open. It was old 50 years ago. I can't imagine the shape it is in today.

Over the years, I have received many comments about my sense of humour. Many have been positive, but I have also heard, "Sarcasm is the ugly cousin of anger." I prefer to think of it as wit! Laughing and making people laugh has been an enjoyable part of my life.

I believe our unusual sense of humour came to Canada from Norway. Bestapa went to the doctor not long before he passed away in 1970. The doctor asked him when he had last seen a doctor. Bestapa said, "June 27." "You mean June 27th," said the doctor. "No," said Bestapa, "June 1927." In other words, he had not seen a doctor in 57 years and then only because he needed clearance to leave Norway for Canada. Humour I appreciate, but not necessarily everyone does, especially that doctor.

As I reflect on my days on the farm, I can't thank Mom enough for the sign, "Don't Worry. It May Never Happen." Farmers came to the prairies so they could own land, and then they left the land, because they couldn't afford to stay on the land. When I left the farm, I always stopped to help people. Then I quit stopping but felt guilty. Now I just drive by them. Trust is gone.

There was joy in the simple life on the farm. However, the simple life resulted in no exposure or knowledge of family violence, alcohol abuse, dangers of smoking, the plight of people on Reserves and issues of sexuality did nothing to solve them.

When you are not aware of problems you don't attempt to resolve them and Dad was right when he said, "If you have five good friends, you have four more than many." You are never poor if you compare to those with less, not more. If you can't be yourself in work or social environments, something should change. I never got involved with something with the intent of losing. Having said that, it resulted in me not doing many things.

I am thankful I learned to enjoy my solitude and accept the things I can't change. It was an eye-opener the day I learned the saying, "Ignorance is bliss," is actually, "If ignorance is bliss, 'tis folly to be wise." Quite a different message.

Success is judged by what you do—not what you say. At age fifteen, a simple "no" rather than submitting to peer pressure could have saved me the cost of cigarettes for 40 years and a heart attack. After high school, in my opinion, I was not well prepared to meet the "outside world" with knowledge but was prepared with character.

I'm now in my seventh decade and feel blessed to be able to share my thoughts with you. I hope you learned something of value.

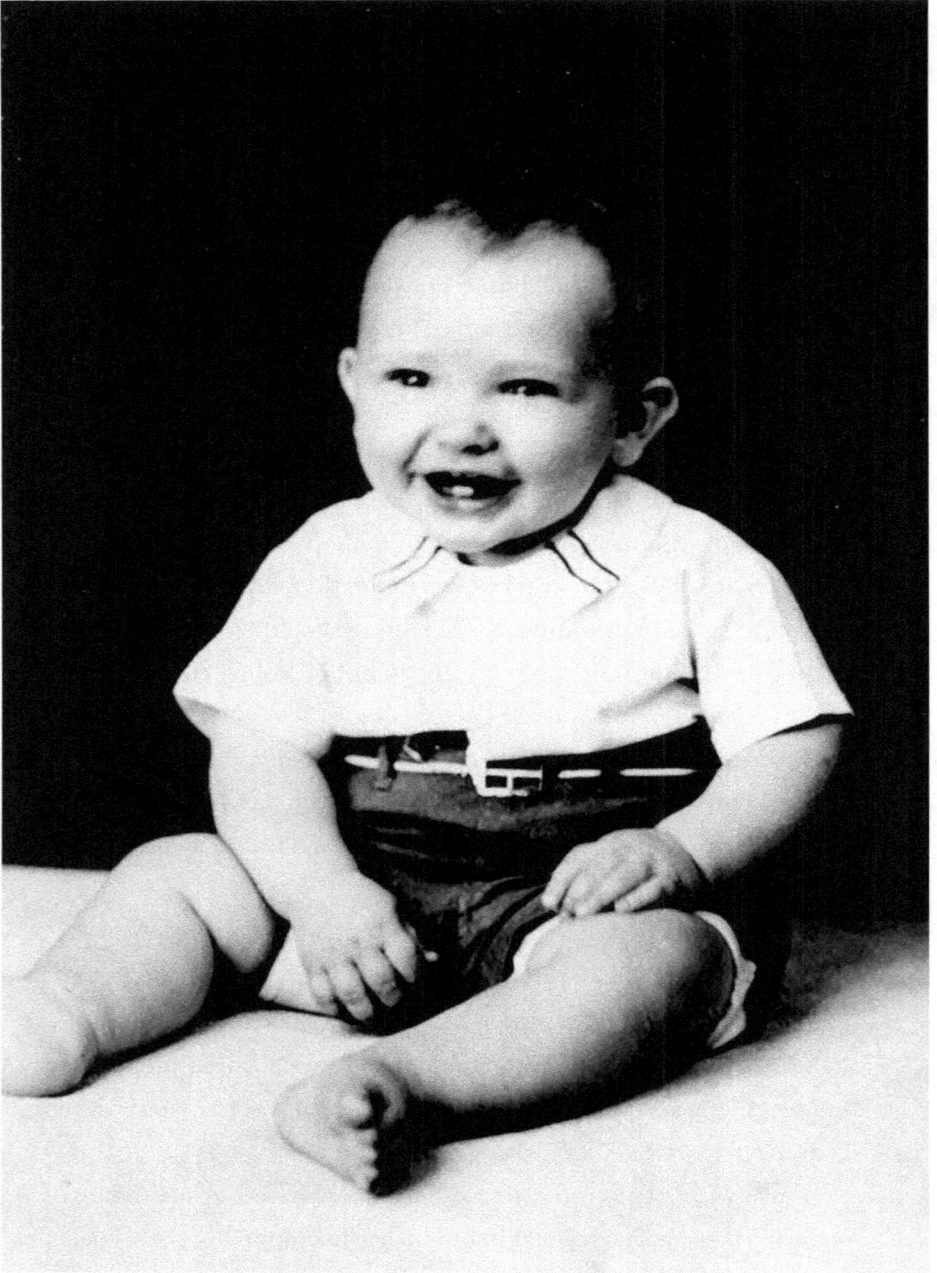

Baby picture of Brian

Brian with award-winning 4H grain plot

Brian with Tippy

Brian graduates with a Bachelor of Education thanks to opportunities

www.ingramcontent.com/pod-product-compliance
Lightning Source LLC
Chambersburg PA
CBHW072008060426
42446CB00042B/2237

* 9 7 8 1 9 9 9 4 4 1 8 6 9 *